Site List

W9-CHB-144

The Wright Places in California

PASADENA	ALICE MILLARD HOUSE
LOS ANGELES	ALINE BARNSDALL HOUSE *
LOS ANGELES	CHARLES ENNIS HOUSE *
HOLLYWOOD	SAMUEL FREEMAN HOUSE
HOLLYWOOD	JOHN STORER HOUSE
BEVERLY HILLS	ANDERTON COURT SHOPS +
BRENTWOOD	GEORGE D. STURGES HOUSE
MALIBU	ARCH OBOLER STUDIO & GATEHOUSE
MONTECITO	GEORGE C. STEWART HOUSE
SAN LUIS OBISPO	KENDERT MEDICAL CLINIC +
CARMEL	CLINTON WALKER HOUSE
PALO ALTO	PAUL and JEAN HANNA HOUSE *
SAN FRANCISCO	V. C. MORRIS GIFT SHOP +
SAN RAFAEL	MARIN COUNTY CIVIC CENTER * +
BERKELEY	HILARY and JOE FELDMAN HOUSE
REDDING	PILGRIM CONGREGATIONAL CHURCH +

The Wright Places in Arizona

PHOENIX	ARIZONA BILTMORE HOTEL *+
	FIRST CHRISTIAN CHURCH *
	NORMAN LYKES HOUSE
	DAVID WRIGHT HOUSE
TEMPE	GRADY GAMMAGE MEMORIAL AUDITORIUM *
SCOTTSDALE	TALIESIN WEST *

* Sites where scheduled or special tours are offered.
+ Buildings generally open to the public .

FINDING THE
WRIGHT PLACES
IN CALIFORNIA
AND ARIZONA

Henry J. Michel

One Palm Books
Los Angeles, California

FINDING THE WRIGHT PLACES
IN CALIFORNIA AND ARIZONA

Copyright © 2000 by Henry J. Michel.
All rights reserved. No part of this book may be repor-
duced in any manner without written consent of the
copyright owner.

Book and cover design by Andy Chase.

Library of Congress Control Number 00-131636
ISBN Number 0-9652237-3-6

Printed in the United States of America

ONE PALM BOOKS is an imprint of
MICHEL PUBLISHING SERVICES
Sherman Oaks, California
onepalmbks@aol.com

Explanation of
Codes, Abbreviations, and Data

Roads

I–xx   Interstate Highway
US xx Numbered U.S. Highway
SR xx Numbered State Route
(xx) County road numbers

In order to show important details
of the routings, maps may not
necessarily depict distances to scale.

Legend

R Right turn
L Left turn
▲ Frank Lloyd Wright site

Fractional miles are
shown in tenths (0.4, 1.3).

Additional Information

Each residence is identified by the name of Wright's client; the public
buildings by their original names.

The dating of each building is based on several widely available sources
which sometimes offer conflicting dates. Some sources may denote the
completion date while others may refer to design date. Dates presented
herein are those more likely to denote when the building was essentially
completed.

Table Of Contents

Redding

Wright In Arizona

San Francisco
Bay Area
see P.54 map

Carmel

San Luis Obispo

Montecito
(atSanta Barbara)

Los Angeles
Area see P.10 map

Wright In California

The first Wright structure in California was of *Prairie House* design, erected at Montecito in 1909. Ten years passed before another Wright house rose in California. Oddly, it was while he was totally occupied for five years with the Imperial Hotel in Tokyo that his major work in California began. A commission from Aline Barnsdall of Los Angeles resulted in *Hollyhock House* and two guest houses, completed while he was still in Japan.

Upon his return, Wright executed four commissions in the Los Angeles area. These were his concrete *textile block* houses involving the experimental use of concrete as a residential building material. He sought, unsuccessfully, to establish a practice in Los Angeles; then went back to his Wisconsin home. Later he returned to the Southwest, builing a new home and studio for himself in the desert east of Phoenix - his *Taliesin West*. In time, commissions in both Arizona and California came his way.

Frank Lloyd Wright's California residences range from his earlier *Prairie* style to versions of his much-later utilitarian *Usonian* homes. In non-residential works he created three commercial structures, a church and the massive Marin County Civic Center complex, completed after his death.

There are a total of twentyfour sites in California with Wright-designed structures.* Clustered mainly in the Los Angles and San Francisco Bay areas, they comprise the largest concentration of his works outside of the Midwest.

*(Some of the private residences are ommited from this guide because of their limited viewing access.)

Visiting the California Sites

This guide to buildings in California and Arizona designed by Frank Lloyd Wright is equally useful whether you are a visitor from afar or you reside near any of the sites.

While the Arizona section is presented as a tour of six closely located sites, the sixteen California sites are shown individually. You can visit them singly or arranged in whatever group or order best fits with your recreational or travel plans.

In the California section, maps and directions relate each site to the closest freeways or main highways. From there the way is shown, street by street, to each location. In the Los Angeles or San Francisco Bay areas, you should fit your approach to the mapped areas according to your own location or travel route.

The directions are designed to give the easiest (and usually shortest) route to each site. Attention was given to usually prevailing traffic conditions and to key "navigating markers" to aid the driver along the way. Nevertheless, a California road map and street maps of the metropolitan areas can give added assistance.

Several sites offer guided tours. Tour days and hours may vary by season and can change or be suspended. To avoid disappointment, you should verify by phone before traveling to a site.

Some private residences are listed in the guide. Their inclusion does not imply that visitors may intrude. Please respect the private nature of these sites, all of which can be viewed and photographed from the roadside.

Information on visiting the Arizona sites starts on page 79.

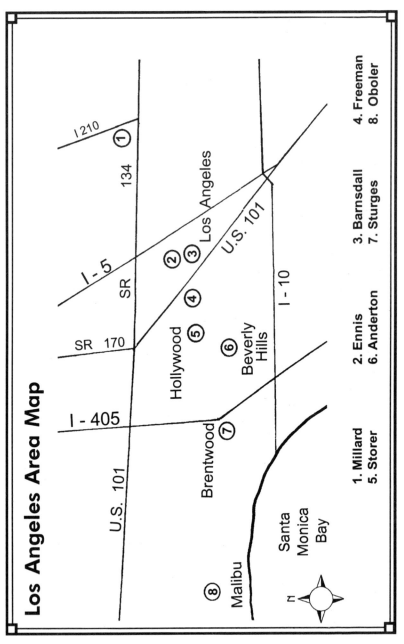

Los Angeles Area Map

I 210

① 134

I - 5

SR

Los Angeles

U.S. 101

② ③

④

⑤

⑥

Hollywood

Beverly Hills

I - 10

SR 170

I - 405

⑦

Brentwood

U.S. 101

⑧ Malibu

Santa Monica Bay

N

1. Millard
5. Storer

2. Ennis
6. Anderton

3. Barnsdall
7. Sturges

4. Freeman
8. Oboler

Alice Millard House

1923

"La Miniatura"

□□□ This house, set in a shallow ravine, is Wright's first experiment in residential concrete clock. The Millards had been earlier clients in Illinois. Now widowed, Mrs. Millard wanted a small house and library to house her large and valuable book collection.

Plain, patterned, and perforated (to allow light) blocks serve as interior as well as exterior walls and hint at Wright's liking for Mayan designs. His plan for an adjacent library proved too costly for the client. In 1926 one of stucco, trimmed with concrete blocks, was added by Lloyd Wright (see p.76).□□□

Alice Millard House

645 Prospect Crescent - Pasadena

LOCATION - Pasadena is about ten miles northeast of downtown Los Angeles.

DIRECTIONS - From I-210 (Foothill Fwy) West - Pick up 134 Fwy briefly, then exit at Orange Gove Blvd. and turn **R** onto Orange Grove. Go north 0.7 mi. to Rosemont Ave. Continue north 1 blk. and turn **L** at the stone-pillared entrance of Prospect Blvd. Drive about 0.5 mi. to Prospect Crescent, turn **L** and the house is in view.
From SR-134 (Ventura Fwy) East - Exit at Orange Grove Blvd. and turn **L** and proceed 0.7 mi. on Orange Grove to Rosemont Ave. Continue north 1 blk.: turn **L** at stone-pillared entrance of Prospect Blvd. Drive about 0.5 mi. to Prospect Crescent, turn **L** and the house is in view.

ACCESSIBILITY - This is a private residence. View the front from Prospect Crs. Seen from Rosemont is the studio and pond.

PARKING - O.K. on Prospect Crs. but not on Rosemont. Use Prospect Terrace, just to the north, and walk a block down Rosemont.

PHOTOGRAPHY - Good views of facade and entrance areas, but difficult to shoot the back from the Rosemont side. Telephoto lens can help.

Alice Millard House

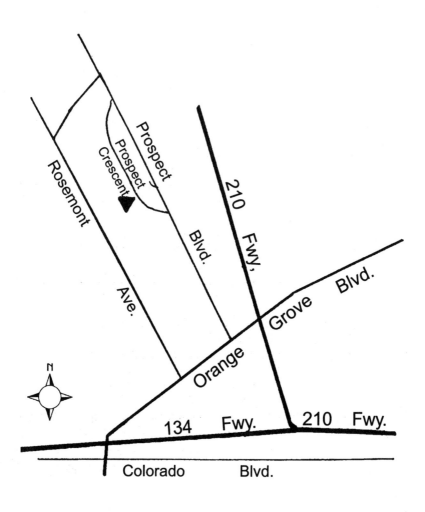

The short CAMEO pieces in this book touch upon both the personal and professional life of the architect. While a mere sampling of the many tales written about the man, these anecdotal stories provide interesting glimpses into Wright's long, complex life. We hope they serve as a stimulant for both active and armchair travelers to visit some Wright -designed buildings.

Cameo 1

Frank Lloyd Wright's father, William Carey Wright, was a man with a facile mind and many talents, yet he was unable to establish and maintain a successful family life. He and his wife, Anna, separated when Frank was in his teens. His uncles and aunts, the Lloyd Jones clan of his mother's side, provided the young boy a measure of family stability that was lacking in his own family.

Wright tells us his mother prenatally willed him to be a builder, later exposing his young mind to architectural etchings and indoctrinating him in the elements of shape, texture and color with a set of Froebel educational toys. How much of Wright's genius can be credited to inherited genes (or to the mystical wishing of his mother) no one can say. That he developed the ability to totally visualize spatial relationships within entire structures is a certainty.

Aline Barnsdall House
1921

"Hollyhock House"

□□□Wright called it a *California Romanza*. This stucco-walled house is liberally trimmed with concrete. His stylized rendition of the client's favorite flower, the hollyhock (giving the house its name), is seen throughout the house in cast concrete.

The many terraces (roof-top included) evidence Wright's appreciation of the mild Southern California climate and the penchant of the region's residents for outdoor-living. In Wright's absence, job supervision was by architect Rudolf Schindler and Wright's son Lloyd.□□□

Aline Barnsdall House

4808 Hollywood Blvd. - Los Angeles

LOCATION - In Barnsdall Art Park near the intersection of Hollywood Blvd. and Vermont Ave, just east of Hollywood.

DIRECTIONS - From US 101 (Hollywood Fwy.) -
North: Exit Vermont Ave., turn **R**, go 1.5 mi. to Hollywood Blvd. turn **L**. Park entrance is at left about 1 block west.
South: Exit Hollywood Blvd., turn **L**, go 1.5 mi. to park entrance just past Edgemont Ave. Turn **R** into park.
From I-5 (Golden State Fwy.) -
North or South: Exit Los Feliz Blvd. turn west, go 2.25 mi. to Vermont Ave., south 0.5 mi. to Hollywood Blvd., turn **R**. Park entrance is on the left about 1 block west.

PARKING - Free in designated Art Park parking areas.

ACCESSIBILITY - The hourly guided tours, Wed. through Sun. noon to 3 p.m., will be discontinued in 2000 when a two-year-long repair and restoration program begins. During that time an exterior tour and an interpretive display at the adjacent Municipal Art Gallery will be offered. Call for current information:
House- (323) 913-4157 or Art Gallery- (213) 485-4581

The adjacent guest house now serves as the Barnsdall Art Center and is not open to tours (see p. 75).

PHOTOGRAPHY - Interior and exterior photography is allowed.

Aline Barnsdall House

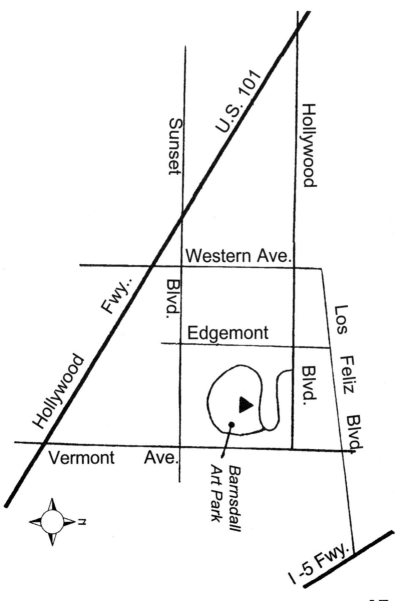

U.S. 101

Sunset

Hollywood

Western Ave.

Fwy.

Blvd.

Edgemont

Los Feliz Blvd.

Blvd.

Hollywood

Vermont Ave.

Barnsdall Art Park

I-5 Fwy.

N

Cameo 2

The Lloyd Jones clan had come to Wisconsin from Wales in the 1840s and settled along the Wisconsin River fifty miles west of Madison, the state capitol. They spawned a progeny that was to leave its mark in several fields and in many parts of the country.

Frank Lloyd Wright himself physically left his architectural stamp in thirty-five states, plus Canada and Japan. But the descendants of the clan were not limited to a single shining star. His two oldest sons became architects. Lloyd Wright, the elder, left a body of distinctive work, much of it in California.

There were others in his mother's family line who shone in other fields. An uncle was a prominent Unitarian minister in Chicago and Wisconsin. Two aunts established a well known co-educational boarding school. A cousin, Richard Lloyd Jones, became a newspaper editor and publisher in Tulsa, Oklahoma. Wright's son, Robert, was a successful lawyer in Washington, D. C. His granddaughter, was Oscar-winning actress Anne Baxter.

There seemed to be few limits to the areas in which the family could excel.

Charles Ennis House
1924

□□□ This is the largest and most complex of Wright's four California *textile block* houses. Extensive use of glass (including Wright's last art glass designs - 39 panels) give it a light, open feeling, with grand views of the city below and mountains to the east.

When the client insisted on selecting much of the interior materials, Wright bowed out, leaving his son, Lloyd, to finish the job. A later owner called Wright back for some alterations, but the. Ennises choices of tile and marble remain.

Now called the Ennis-Brown House, it is run by a non-profit trust that is dedicated to its perpetual care and to its presentation to the public as an example of Wright's unique work in the Los Angeles area.□□□

19

Charles Ennis House

2607 Glendower Ave. - Los Angeles

LOCATION - The house is near the Greek Theater section of Griffith Park, between the I-5 and US 101 freeways. Hollyhock House is juat a mile to the south.

DIRECTIONS - (See map on page 17 for approaches to the area.) **From the Vermont Ave.-Los Feliz Blvd. intersection**, proceed north on Vermont to the second street, Cromwell, then turn **L** across the center parkway. Directly ahead, Glendower Rd. starts up the hill. Turn **R** and stay on Glendower Road for 0.6 mi. to the address.

PARKING - Street parking is very limited and restricted in many places. Scheduled visitors will receive instructions.

ACCESSIBILITY - Tours are by reservation only. This residence offers public tours on the second Saturday in Jan., Mar., May, July. Sept. and Nov. The fee includes shuttle service from a designated nearby parking area - $10 adults, $5 seniors, students, youngsters (child in arms free). Call 323-668-0234 for information and reservation. Special tours for schools, groups and out-of-town visitors may be arranged.

PHOTOGRAPHY - Several aspects of the exterior can be shot from spots along the road. Tours allow exterior photography only. Special photography tours by appointment.

Charles Ennis House

Cameo 3

Frank Lloyd Wright was exposed to design and construction work while quite young. Employed as a clerk by a builder who was also dean of the engineering school at the university in Madison, he enrolled in a few classes, including some engineering.

When his minister uncle contemplated erecting a family chapel near Spring Green, Frank submitted a design, but the uncle retained a Chicago architect. Undiscouraged, when construction started Frank was on hand to help and actually designed some interior features. Later he was to learn his craft as most others did in those times; as an apprentice.

He soon became head draftsman under the legendary Chicago architect, Louis H. Sullivan, his mentor. Both were adamant in a desire to perfect an American architecture - unlik the older European styles. When the head of a large architectural firm offered to pay Frank's way through the Ecole des Beaux-Arts in Paris, with a job waiting for him upon return, Wright turned the offer down. He had no interest in working in the classical styles.

Samuel Freeman House
1924

□□□ The smallest of Wright's *textile block* houses. Abundant use of perforated blocks and the unusual corner window designs provide openness and light in this house which is perched on the edge of a steep hill overlooking Los Angeles.

Now in the hands of University of Southern California's architectural department, this gem is in dire need of extensive repairs due to earthquake damage and general deterioration.

Rudolf Schindler, who had supervised construction of Wright's Barnsdall structures (see p. 15), was commissioned by the Freemans to design much of the built-in and free-standing furniture for the house.□□□

23

Samuel Freeman House

1962 Glencoe Way. - Hollywood

LOCATION - In Hollywood near the intersection of Highland Ave. and Hollywood Blvd, about a quarter mile south of the Hollywood Bowl, off US 101.

DIRECTIONS - From US 101 (Hollywood Fwy) -
South: Exit onto Highland Ave., proceed 0.5 mi., get into far right lane which must turn **R** onto Franklin Ave. First street after turn is Hillcrest Ave. A right turn leads to Glencoe Way, two blocks up a steep hill. (See PARKING information below.)
North: Exit at Caheunga Blvd., turn **L** go one block to Franklin Ave. then **R**. Proceed west until Franklin meets Highland and jogs ½ block south. Move into far right lane to return to Franklin turning **R**. First street after turn is Hillcrest Ave. A right turn leads to Glencoe Way, two blocks up a steep hill. (See PARKING information.)

PARKING - On the steep streets north of Franklin parking is very limited. Consider using the streets below Franklin with time limit or meter parking. If walking is a problem, drive up, turn around where Glencoe makes a sharp left in front of the Freeman House, (Do not drive beyond this point). Park facing downhill on Glencoe or Hillcrest.

ACCESSIBILITY and PHOTOGRAPHY - Tours have been discontinued indefinitely. Views of the exterior are quite limited. You can approach and photograph the north face and entrance terrace on Glencoe Way. From streets below the hill (Franklin, Highland), the house can be seen with binoculars or photographed with a fairly powerful telephoto lens.

Samuel Freeman House

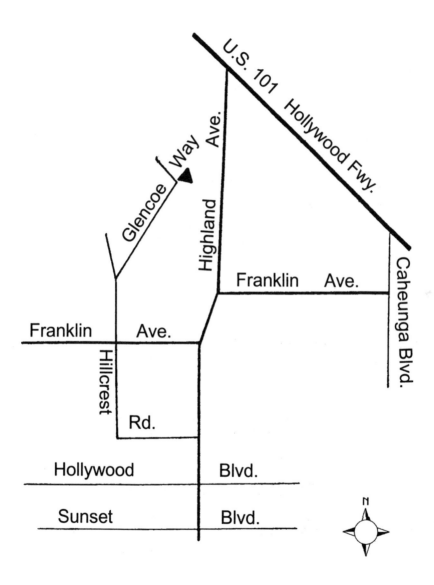

Cameo 4

When Wright left Madison, intent on becoming an architect in Chicago, he had virtually no formal training and minimal experience in construction. He used his acquaintanceship with his uncle's architect, Joseph Silsbee, to enter the profession. Silsbee hired him as a tracer at $ 8 a week, which was soon raised to $ 12.

When Wright asked for another raise, Silsbee balked, so he left and talked his way into another firm at a $ 15 salary; He found the job was beyond him, so he went to his old employer and, using his new pay as a measure of his worth, offered to return. He was soon back with Silsbee at the higher pay. But he was uninspired by the Queen Anne style Silsbee was known for and began looking to work else-where.

There was an opening in the prestigious firm of Adler and Sullivan. Wright hurried over with a portfolio of his work. Sullivan was impressed and hired him .It was the real beginning of his career. In less than two years he was head draftsman. Sullivan called him :"the pencil in my hand." He referred to Sullivan as his "lieber meister." Until their later break-up, there was almost a father-son relationship.

Wright's game-playing with Silsbee and his aggressive tactics in forging ahead show his mind-set which he later put so frankly in his own words: "Early on I had to choose between honest arrogance and hypocritical humility. I chose arrogance."

John Storer House

1923-24

□□□ The second of Wright's California *textile block* houses uses perforated blocks and floor-to-ceiling glass panels between the two-story- tall block columns of the living room to allow daylight to flood the rooms. Perched on a hillside site that gives it sweeping views of the city, the house presents an imposing facade.

The recently added security wall along the street was carefully designed to match the original blocks of the house. □□□

John Storer House

8161 Hollywood Blvd. — Hollywood

LOCATION — At the west end of Hollywood where Hollywood Blvd. is a curvy, residential street in the hills west of Laurel Canyon Blvd.

DIRECTIONS — From US 101 North — Exit Sunset Blvd. and proceed west 3.0 mi. *or* US 101 South — Exit Vine St., **R** 3 blk. to Sunset, turn **R**, go west 2.2 mi.
Then:
At Cresecent Heights Blvd. go one block beyond to Selma Ave. and turn **R**. Drive 0.2 mi. to Crescent Hts. where a sharp left sends you up around two curves to Hollywood Blvd. (It may be unsigned). Turn **R**, go about 100 yds. and **R** again. The house is directly in front of you. (Note: Approach via Hollywood Blvd. from the east is not recommended.)
Coming from the north, you can use Laurel Canyon Blvd. As you exit the hills, shunt to the right onto Hollywood Blvd., up the ramp-like street, around a curve or two and the house is right there.

PARKING — On the street.

ACCESSIBILITY — This is a private residence.

PHOTOGRAPHY — Offers a virtually unobstructed view of the facade from the street.

John Storer House

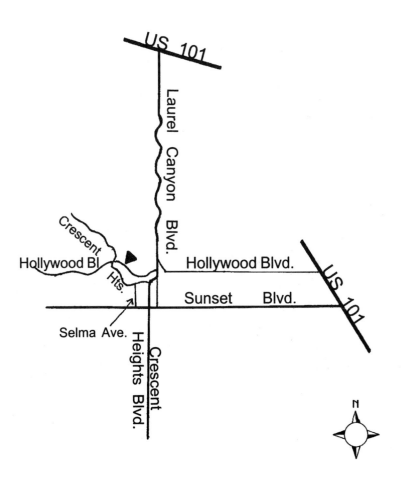

Cameo 5

As the top draftsman in one of the prime architectural firms in the city, the young Wright began to develop socially. He joined clubs and kept company with other up-and-coming young men in the profession. He also attended the social functions of his minister uncle's large and active church. Here he met Catherine Tobin, a young, educated girl from a prosperous Chicago family. Frank began courting "Kitty".

There was soon talk of marriage. The parents, both his and hers, were hesitant to approve because of the couple's youth. Catherine was sent out of town for several months. But Wright persisted and in June 1889 the wedding took place. Catherine was barely 18; Frank not quite 22.

With a loan from his employer, Wright secured a plot in Oak Park, ten miles west of downtown Chicago, were he built his first home. The first two off-springs were boys: Frank Lloyd Jr. (always called Lloyd) and John, both of whom followed in their father's profession. Two girls and two more boys completed the family.

The Wrights lived the life of prosperous suburbanites in that era's developing Chicago metropolis, with Catherine involved in local activities and Frank active in clubs and social functions, and enjoying the theater and his new passion - the automobile .

== The Frank Lloyd Wright Home and Studio, other nearby Wright-designed houses, and his Unity Temple can be visited. For information write to: Oak Park Visitors Center, 158 Forest Avenue, Oak Park, IL 60302 or call 312-848-1500. = =

Anderton Court Shops
1952

□□□ Wright often used ramps to move people in public buildings. He connects floor levels by their use here. The serrated pylon resembles the one on his Marin County Civic Center. His use of the circle, which can be seen in some of the shop windows, is characteristic only of the later part of his career. □□□

Anderton Court Shops

332 Rodeo Drive - Beverly Hills

LOCATION - Beverly Hills is about eight miles west of the Los Angeles Civic Center.

DIRECTIONS- The map locates the 300 block of Rodeo Dr. between Dayton and Brighton. Be alert to No Turn signs and One Way traffic. Here are approaches to the area:
From the I-405 (San Diego Fwy) - (1) Exit at Sunset Blvd., drive east to Beverly Dr., turn **R**, continue past Santa Monica Blvd. to streets shown on map. or - **(2)** Exit at Wilshire Blvd., drive east to the 9600 block as shown.
From the I-10 (Santa Monica Fwy) - Exit at La Cienega Blvd., drive north to Wilshire, turn **L** (west) and go to the 9600 block and the streets shown on map.

PARKING - During business hours parking may be difficult. With luck you can park behind the Court Shops. There is metered parking on most streets, free off-street city-owned lots in the area and private lots too.

ACCESSIBILITY - You can wander through the Court's passageways even before or after shopping hours.

PHOTOGRAPHY - To get just the architecture without the obstructing traffic, early morning (especially Sunday) is a good time. But natural light is best on the facade in late afternoon.

Anderton Court Shops

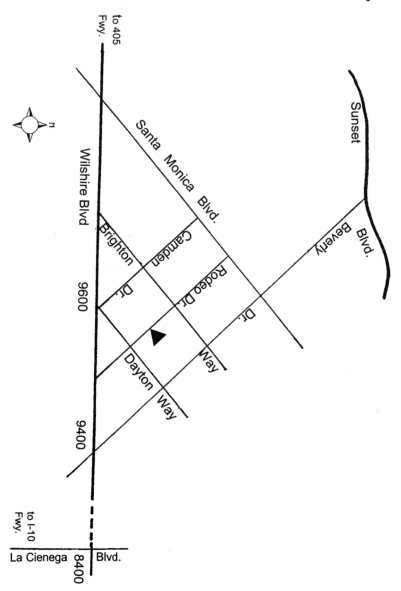

Cameo 6

Wright had the good fortune to work for Louis Sullivan's firm when it designed and built the Auditorium Building (1886-89) on Michigan Avenue in Chicago, It was the first multi-use building of its kind, containing hotel, offices, and theater. The firm of Adler and Sullivan proudly moved to the top floor of its office tower, then the highest structure in the city. Now Wright, a newcomer from provincial Wisconsin, could daily overlook the burgeoning metropolis. It must have nourished his ego with a feeling that he was now on top of the world.

Adler and Sullivan received a commission to design the Transportation Pavilion for Chicago's Colombian Exposition of 1893. This world fair aimed to celebrate the four hundredth anniversary of the discovery of the New World, yet the powers in charge decided to house it in old world architectural styles. But the defiant Sullivan eschewed domes and Doric columns. His was the only major building that did not adhere to the Renaissance style used in all other pavilions. The maverick Sullivan was well suited to be mentor for the soon-to-be radical pioneer of American architecture.

At this exposition Wright saw examples of Japanese art and Mayan architecture, both of which influenced much of his later work.

== The Auditorium Building still stands at the corner of Michigan Ave. and Congress St. and now houses Roosevelt University. Tours are available. ==

George D. Sturges House
1939

□□□ The cube-like structure, suspended out from the hillside slope, is a stunning sight. The brick base growing out of the hill supports the superstructure with its cantilevered terrace enclosed by rough redwood walls. □□□

George D. Sturges House

449 Skyeway Road. — Brentwood

LOCATION — Brentwood is located in the northwest corner of the Los Angeles basin, just west of the 405 Fwy. and about two miles north of the I-10.

DIRECTIONS — From I-405 (San Diego Fwy) – Exit at Sunset Blvd. and go west on Sunset 1 mi. Turn **R** onto Kenter Ave. and drive 0.7 mi. to where Bonhill Rd. and Skyeway Rd. meet Kenter. Best approach is up Bonhill to where it meets Skyeway again. A sharp **R** turn puts you on the side of Skyewiay where parking is allowed. The house is just a few yards past the turn.

PARKING — Street parking is OK on the west (downhill traffic) side of Skyewiay but not the other side in this block.

ACCESSIBILITY — This is a private residence. Much of the exterior, however, can be viewed from the road.

PHOTOGRAPHY — This spectacular structure, projecting from its hillside site can be shot from many angles along the inclined street.

George D. Sturges House

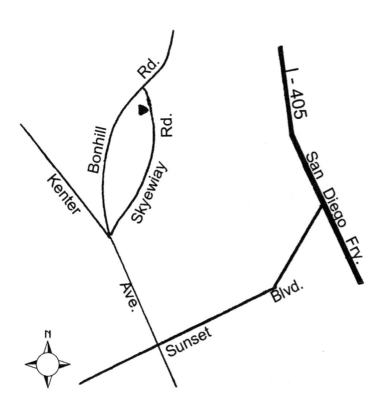

Cameo 7

It was the holiday season. Wright's two boys, Lloyd and John were taken by their maternal grandmother to a Christmas show in downtown Chicago. Fire started in the stage lighting. The asbestos curtain failed to lower and pandemonium ensued.

The Iroquois Theater fire in 1903 took the lives of over six hundred people, most of them up in the balcony. The boys and their grandmother were swept out in the surging main floor mob; separated, but safe.

Fires were to dog Wright throughout his life. Taliesin, his Wisconsin home, was set ablaze by a crazed servant who then set about killing the fleeing occupants with an ax as they tried to escape the conflagration. Murdered were four of his employees and his lover and her two young children. Taliesin was rebuilt, and after a second fire destroyed most of it, was rebuilt again.

Fire also struck in Japan. Returning from an evening's drive, Wright saw smoke coming from his hotel. A valuable collection of art stored in his quarters might have been destroyed. But his friend, Miriam Noel, who became his second wife, had a premonition and had remained behind that evening. She was able to move the art work to safety.

It seems ironic that Wright, who centered his early designs around the fireplace as the focal point of family life, should so often be plagued by flames.

Arch Oboler Gatehouse and Studio

1941

□□□ The famous radio and screen writer of the '30s and '40s did not finish his planned estate. The main house, *Eaglefeather,* to be perched on the ridge of a mountain with a view of the Pacific ocean was not built.

Only the studio-retreat (above) and the gatehouse (p. 76) were completed. Built of rubblestone-embedded concrete and redwood walls, the two buildings are superb examples of Wright's skill in mating structure with site. This long-neglected property will be benefiting from some restorative measures by its new owner. □□□

39

Arch Oboler Gatehouse and Studio

32436 Mulholland Hwy. — Malibu

LOCATION — In the mountains high above the famed Malibu coastal colony, the Oboler site is more easily approached by the inland route via US 101. It is some 37 miles northwest of the Los Angeles Civic Center, about 6 miles south of Westlake Village.

DIRECTIONS – From US 101 North or South — Exit onto Westlake Blvd. (SR 23), proceed south through Westlake Village for five miles to juncture with Mulholland Hwy. Turn **L** (east) onto Mulholland and drive 1.5 mi. to address on the mail box where the gatehouse can be seen across a narrow ravine. From a spot about 500 yards up the road one sees the studio high on a peak.
As An Alternate Route — If starting from coastal areas west of Los Angeles, you may wish to use Pacific Coast Hwy. and either Mulholland or SR 23 (Decker Rd.).

PARKING — Roadside parking where the shoulder allows. The traffic is light, but fast vehicles dictate caution.

ACCESSIBILITY — This private property can be viewed from the road.

PHOTOGRAPHY — For the studio a telephoto lens is needed. Early morning is best, as later shadows and back lighting obliterate details.

Arch Oboler Gatehouse and Studio

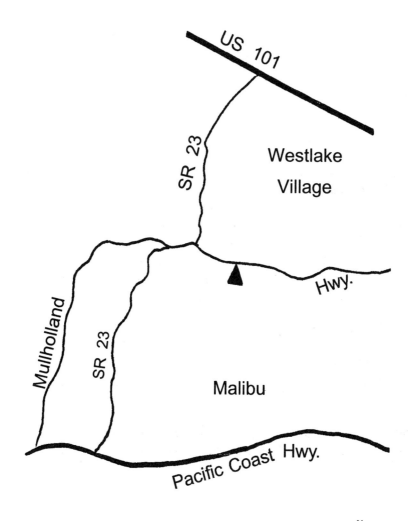

US 101

SR 23

Westlake

Village

Mullholland

SR 23

Hwy.

Malibu

Pacific Coast Hwy.

N

Cameo 8

Wright's tastes and interests changed once he left the prosaic life of small city and farm to become a young man in a bustling, growing Chicago. He acquired a liking for the theatre and the lifestyle of the fashionably dressed man-about-town.

Later, he began to attire himself in a highly personal style, often bordering on the bizarre. The beret, the cloak, walking stick and the flat-crowned broad-brimmed hat were aimed to set himself apart as an artist.

Mechanical things held a facination for him. In Oak Park, he owned one of the first cars in town. Towns-people dubbed the speedster the "yellow devil." Latter Wright favored larger vehicles like the Packard phaeton he painted Cherokee red, his favorite color.

An incurable spendthrift, he indulged himself in objects d'art and expensive furnishings. To accommodate to an irregular and often non-existent income, he resorted to ignoring his debts until he was hounded or squeezed by his creditor. He borrowed from well-to-do clients or friends and was more than once close to bankruptcy and in danger of losing Taliesin, his home. Even in the later years, when his numerous commissions would have allowed him to live in copious comfort, he still overspent in order to maintain a somewhat ostenta-tious lifestyle.

George C. Stewart House

1909

□□□ This first Wright-designed home built in California was for an earlier Midwest client, and it echoes Wright's Prairie style. He was not involved in its construction and it has been much modified over the years. Its redwood exterior lends a Craftsman-like touch to what in brick and stone would have suited it for a site facing Lake Michigan rather than the Pacific, a view now obscured by giant trees. □□□

George C. Stewart House

196 Hot Springs Road — Montecito

LOCATION — Montecito is located just south of Santa Barbara on US 101.

DIRECTIONS — From US 101 North – Use the Olive Mill Rd./Coastal Village Rd. exit ramp, Go straight ahead onto Coastal Village Rd., 0.7 mi. to Hot Springs Rd. and turn **R** then a short distance (past Palm Tree Ln. and Hermosilla Dr.) up to Summit Rd. Turn **R** on Summit; the house is at your right.

From US 101 South — Use Hot Springs Rd./Coastal Village Rd. exit. At end of ramp turn **L** onto Hot Springs Rd. a short distance (past Palm Tree Ln. and Hermosilla Dr.) up to Summit Rd. Turn **R** on Summit; the house is at your right.

PARKING — Park on Summit Rd. There's no parking on Hot Springs Rd.

ACCESSIBILITY — This is a private residence. Viewing is from the street.

PHOTOGRAPHY — There is an unobstructed view of the front of the house from Summit Rd.

George C. Stewart House

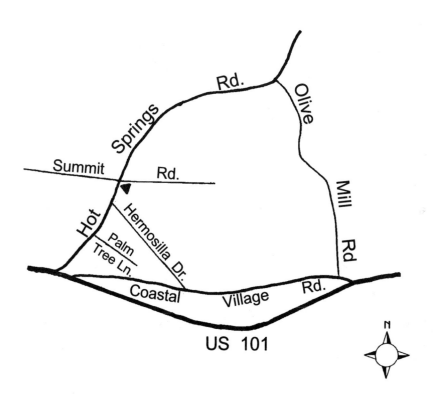

Cameo 9

Frank Lloyd Wright began independent practice out of his Oak Park home after leaving Sullivan in 1893. He went on to gain renown with his "prairie style" residences and larger structures such as Unity Temple in Oak Park. In Chicago he remodeled the lobby of *The Rookery* building and built *Robie House*, his quintessential *Prairie House*. He had a fine practice and considerable fame. At home, the Wrights seemed to be living the life of the typical, prosperous suburban family of those days.

Wright jeopardized it all in 1909 when he left his family to spend a year in Europe, accompanied by the wife of a former client. This caused such a scandal in Oak Park and Chicago that upon return he retreated to the Wisconsin valley of his ancestors and built *Taliesin* which became his home and studio. He continued his relationship with the woman, as his wife refused to secure a divorce.

= *Unity Temple, Wright's Home and Studio, and other homes in Oak Park, Ill. can be seen or toured. In Chicago you can see The Rookery and tour Robie House. Taliesin at Spring Green, Wisconsin is open May to October.* =

Kundert Medical Clinic

1954-56

□□□ Wright's client, Dr. Karl Kundert, retired a good while ago but the building which has benifited from a restoration is now occupied by another doctor.

There is a mix of much of the traditional Wright here - extensive use of brick, flat roof, and patterned clerestory windows. And in the waiting room, like a harkening back to his *Prairie Houses, is* a fireplace. Here it is set in a tall ceiling-high brick wall. □□□

Kundert Medical Clinic

1106 Pacific Street — San Luis Obispo

LOCATION — San Luis Obispo is in the central coastal area midway between Santa Barbara and Monterey on US 101.

DIRECTIONS — From US 101 North - Exit at Marsh St., continue on Marsh 0.8 mi. to Santa Rosa Ave.; turn **R**. Go 1 block to Pacific St. and the building is at the left as you cross the bridge.
From US 101 South - Exit at Monterey St. and continue 0.8 mi. to Santa Rosa Ave. Turn **L** and go three blocks to Pacific St. It is on the corner to your left.

PARKING — Park on the street or in the clinic's lot at the far end of the building.

ACCESSIBILITY — The curent occupants are empathetic with Wright aficionados. When the clinic is open, visitors are welcome to enter and view the reception/waiting area and to sign the visitor log.

PHOTOGRAPHY — All sides of the exterior as well as the waiting room are at your camera's disposal (but waiting patients are entitled to their privacy, please).

Kundert Medical Clinic

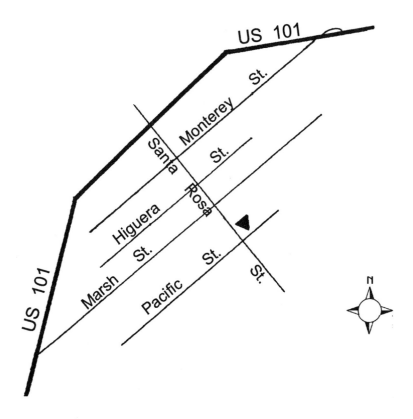

Cameo 10

For nearly twenty years after leaving his Oak Park home and family and settling in Wisconsin, Wright's private life was in continual turbulence. First, he looses his new love in the tragic Taliesin fire of 1914. Then he falls prey to an emotionally unstable stranger who salves his despair in a letter of consolation and sympathy. But later on, the chameleon-like Miriam Noel exhibits fits of erratic behavior and, eventually, a violent antagonism.

The two maintain an uneasy relationship for nine years while Catherine delays getting her divorce. They then marry in 1923 and things become stormier. Within a few months Miriam leaves Wright and begins a three year campaign of harassment and legal attacks that threaten Wright financially.

During this time Wright meets the woman who will become his third wife. She is Olgivanna Milanoff, a descendant of a family of minor aristocrats in eastern Europe. Separated and divorcing, she becomes the mother of Wright's seventh child, Iovanna.

Educated and competent, Olgavanna is involved in many aspects of Wright's life, especially the Taliesin Fellowship, the school they establish at the Wisconsin complex. Olgivanna is the perfect soul-mate; Wright's constant companion for his remaining thirty-five years.

Clinton Walker House

1948

□□□ This stone and glass house with its angular ship-like shapes, set on coastal rocks jutting to the sea, combine for a spectacular sight. The patina-toned, layered metal roof brings to mind the wind-bent cypresses of the Monterey area. □□□

Clinton Walker House

Scenic Road at Santa Lucia Ave. — Carmel

LOCATION — Carmel is on the coast, just south of Monterey, midway between San Francisco and San Luis Obispo, west of Salinas.

DIRECTIONS — From US 101 North — At Salinas take SR 68 West 20 mi. to SR 1. Follow SR 1 about 5 mi. south to Carmel.
From US 101 South — Exit to SR 156 West (at Prunedale). Drive about 7 mi. on 156 which merges with SR 1 beyond Castroville; continue on SR 1 about 17 mi. to Carmel.
From SR 1 — You can enter the north end of Carmel at Carpenter St. or Ocean Ave., then go across town toward Scenic Rd. along the ocean. The house is beyond the end of the beach and park areas just below Santa Lucia Ave. **OR:** continue south on SR 1 to Rio Rd. near the Mission. Turn **R**, go about 0.7 mi. to Santa Lucia Ave. then **L** to Scenic Rd. and **L** again.

PARKING — Allowed on Scenic Rd.

ACCESSIBILITY — This is a private residence.

PHOTOGRAPHY — The house can be shot from either side at road level or, when the tide is out, from various beach-level locations on either side of the promontory. There are stairs to the beach at the north side.

Clinton Walker House

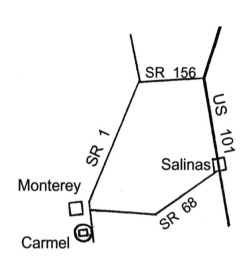

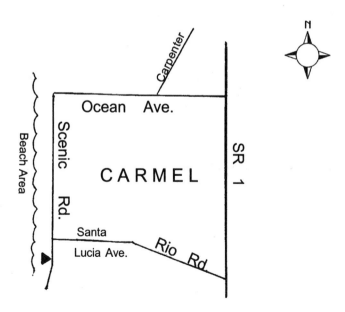

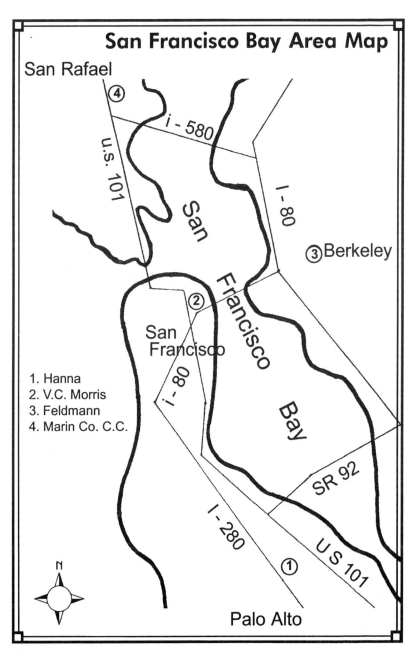

San Francisco Bay Area Map

San Rafael

④

i - 580

u.s. 101

I - 80

San

③Berkeley

Francisco

②

San
Francisco

i - 80

1. Hanna
2. V.C. Morris
3. Feldmann
4. Marin Co. C.C.

Bay

SR 92

I - 280

①

U S 101

N

Palo Alto

Paul and Jean Hanna House

1936

"Honeycomb House" at Stanford University

□□□ Brick terrace walls form a base against the hilside for the lighter openness of the house's glass-panelled walls under nearly flat roofs. Its name derives from the hexagonal module used in its plan.

In a memorial at its 1960 national convention, the American Institute of Architects recommended that this and sixteen others of Wright's buildings be permanently preserved. □□□

Paul and Jean Hanna House

737 Frenchman's Road - Palo Alto

LOCATION - Palo Alto is some 30 miles south of San Francisco via US 101 or I-280. The house is on the Stanford University campus.

DIRECTIONS -From US 101 (Bayshore Fwy) -
North or South: Exit Oregon Expressway (G3), proceed west on Oregon, which in 1 mi. becomes Page Mill Rd. Continue another mile to Junipero Serra Blvd., turn **R** and proceed 1.5 mi. to East Campus Dr.

Enter campus at East Campus Dr. Go 0.5 mi. to Mayfield Ave. and 0.4 mi. to Frenchman's Rd. Drive a block or so on Frenchmen's to a 'Y' in the road and it's on the hill at your left.

From I-280 (Junipero Serra Fwy) North - Exit at Page Mill Rd. (G3), go north 1 mi. to Junipero Serra Blvd., turn **L**, go 1.5 mi. to East Campus Dr. Then follow directions in bold type paragraph above.

From I-280 (Junipero Serra Fwy) South - Exit Sand Hill Rd., go east to Junipero Serra Blvd., turn R, go 0.7 mi. to East Campus Dr. Then follow directions in bold type paragraph above.

PARKING - Tour visitors get parking permits and instructions. Casual visitors should observe posted street signs.

ACCESSIBILITY -Tours, by appointment only, are offered the 1st Sunday (11:00 am) and 2nd and 4th Thursdays (2:00 pm) of each month. Fee is $7.00 a person plus a $2.00 parking permit per vehicle. Call 650-725-8352 well in advance for reservations or for information. Casual visitors can view the front exterior of the house from the road. Binoculars help.

PHOTOGRAPHY - After tours, visitors can shoot exterior and grounds. Casual visitors can get facade from the street. Telephoto lens helps.

Paul and Jean Hanna House

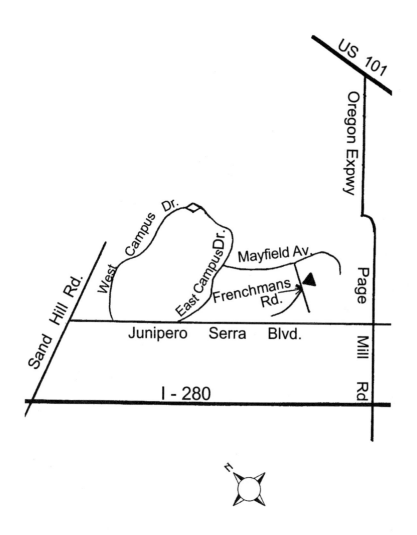

Cameo 11

When the nation's economy slumped in the early 1930s, Wright lost several promising commissions. He was in dire financial straits. As a way of survival he established a school of architecture, the Taliesin Fellowship, hoping that student fees would generate sufficient income and, with what he made through his lectures and writings, he could hold on until the economy improved.

The school was unorthodox and informal in its approach. It was "hands-on" learning from the ground up - including Spartan living, kitchen duty, field and farm work along with building additions to Taliesin. It was learning by doing and by watching the master work. When commissions eventually came, the more capable apprentices served as job supervisors.

Taliesin West, in Scottsdale, Arizona became the Fellowship's winter quarters. Everything shifted seasonally between the Wisconsin and the desert complexes. In the early years each spring and fall saw a caravan of vehicles in a cross-country trek led by Wright in his bright red Packard touring car. Meals were prepared in an improvised kitchen-on-wheels; not unlike the "chuck wagons" of the old cattle drive days in the West.

Now a more formal school exists, but some of the principles of the Taliesin Fellowship survive, It still stresses learning by doing and it still switches its location with the change of seasons.

V. C. Morris Gift Shop

1948

□□□ Wright converted an existing building into this unique space for a retail shop. His use of the arched entryway - seen in some of his early designs - was never more arresting than here where it balances and anchors the tall brick facade rising high above it.

The display space he created with the narrow ramp that clings to and circles the interior walls foreshadows his Guggenheim Museum plan.

It is one of three California buildings cited by the American Institute of Architects as representative of Wright's contribution to American culture.□□□

V. C. Morris Gift Shop

140 Maiden Lane - San Francisco

LOCATION - In the heart of San Francisco, just north of Market St. next to Union Square.

DIRECTIONS - From US 101 North - Transition to I-80 East, take Fourth St. exit onto Bryant, go 1 blk. to Third St., turn **L**. Go 4 blks. to junction of Market and Geary. Maiden Lane is half a block north of there.

From US 101 South - (Off the Golden Gate Bridge 101 is on surface streets.) From Van Ness Ave. (101) turn **L** on Post St. for 0.8 mi. to Stockton St. at Union Square. Maiden Lane is half a block to the south.

From I-80 West - From the East Bay area and beyond, use the San Francisco-Oakland Bay Bridge (I-80) to San Francisco. Exit Fifth St., **R** a block to Folsom St., **R** to Third St. and turn **L**. Go 4 blks. to junction of Market and Geary. Maiden Lane is half a block north of there.

PARKING - Maiden Lane is a restricted/no parking zone. There is metered parking on nearby streets and many fee lots and garages are in the area.

ACCESSIBILITY - Maiden Lane is a two-block-long pedestrian mall. The Shop, now an art gallery, is open during normal shopping hours.

PHOTOGRAPHY - A wide angle lens is best from across the narrow street. Interior shots need approval of the store management.

V. C. Morris Gift Shop

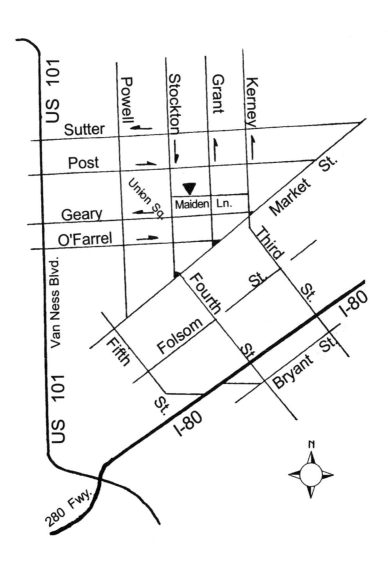

Cameo 12

For the S. C. Johnson Wax Company headquarters in Racine, Wisconsin, Wright designed a very unconventional column to support the three-story-high ceiling above a large, open office area. From a nine inch diameter at its base it increased gradually in size., then flared out at the top like a broad, flat 'lilly-pad"flower.

The building inspectors would not issue permits for their use. Columns that tall, the engineers said. had to be three feet in diameter, Disregarding such technicalities, Wright started construction. Then he erected a prototype of the column and invited officials to watch it be loaded with sand bags and steel beams. The column withstood many times the weight needed for approval. He got his permits.

The Johnson Wax building (along with *Fallingwater* in Pennsylvania) was one of his great successes in the late thirties that started a resurgence of Wright's work and propelled him into two decades of amazing productivity after the age of seventy.

= Tours of the S. C. Johnson Administration Building in Racine Wis. are available on week days by reservation. =

Marin County Civic Center

1957-72

□□□ Containing the county's offices, its central library, the courts and even a jail, the huge two-winged building is set among rolling hills. Designed and begun before Wright's death, the complex was completed under the other architects associated with his *Taliesin West* studio. The Administration Building was finished in 1962; the Hall of Justice in 1969. It is designated a National Historic Landmark.

Across Civic Center Drive is the Civic Center Post Office, Wright's only completed design for the U.S. Government. A quarter mile up the Drive is the Veterans' Memorial Auditorium (1972) which repeats the distinctive roof design of the Civic Center buildings (see p. 77). □□□

63

Marin County Civic Center

3501 Civic Center Drive - San Rafael

LOCATION - San Rafael is 10 mi. north of San Francisco and the Golden Gate Bridge, on US 101.

DIRECTIONS - From US 101 North or South -
Take the N. San Pedro Rd. exit and head east. Turn **L** at first traffic signal east of the freeway; Civic Center Drive. The Center is there at your left.

PARKING - Ample free parking areas surround the building.

ACCESSIBILITY - Exteriors of all structures can be seen at any time. The Civic Center is open during normal business hours, Monday thru Friday. Guided tours are given at 10:30 Wednesday mornings ($3.00 donation suggested). They start from the gift shop at the dining area; second floor of the Hall of Justice wing. To arrange special tours at other times (groups of five or more; fee $3.00), call 415-499-6646.

The small post office building across Civic Center Dr. can be visited during business and open-lobby hours. The Veterans Memorial Auditorium is open only for scheduled events.

PHOTOGRAPHY - This is a subject that will make an amateur photographer's day.

Marin County Civic Center

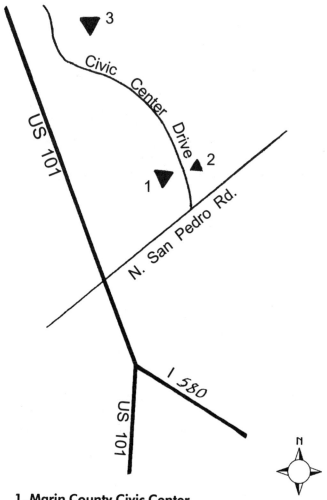

1. Marin County Civic Center
2. San Rafael Post Office
3. Veterans Memorial Auditorium

Cameo 13

Architectural historian Edgar Kaufmann, Jr. was a Taliesin Fellowship student. whose father, a Pittsburgh merchant, asked Wright to design a small country retreat for him. Wright visited the property in mountains southeast of Pittsburgh. It was a rustic, wooded area where the family had spent many summer weekends.

There was a lively stream nearby cascading over a rocky ledge opposite the Kaufmann's old cabin. Wright asked how the family spent their days in these woods and learned that the Kaufmanns often relaxed atop the huge boulder that rose above the stream next to the fall. This led to Wright's positioning of the house.as he did.

Kafmann expected Wright would give him a house with a broad view of the stream and falls, much like their original cabin. But Wright spurned so conventional a location. He designed a house that would overhang the falls and located it so that the tip of the boulder Kaufmann had mentioned protrudes through the living room floor near the fireplace. The boulder, the stream, and the falls were all made an integral part of the house called *Fallingwater*. It is now the most visited residence in the country.

= = Fallingwater is open most of the year. Call 412-329-8501 = =
= = or write to P O Box R, Mill Run, PA 15464 for information = =

Hilary and Joe Feldman House

1974

□□□ Derived from one of Wright's unrealized plans for a Southern California site in the 1930's, this house is perched on a steep slope of the coastal hills in the East Bay area of the San Francisco Bay region.

While the house has characteristics of its earlier origin - a Wright Usonian house design - this 1970s version was made somewhat more elaborate, quite befitting its cliff-like, bay-view site. □□□

Hilary and Joe Feldman House

13 Mosswood Road. — Berkeley

LOCATION — Berkeley is just north of Oakland on the east side of San Francisco Bay.

DIRECTIONS — The key approach route is Interstate 80, reachable from all directions via the various connector links around the Bay area (280, 580, 880, etc.) depending on your line of approach.
From I-80 along the East Bay coast — Exit University Ave. and go east 2 mi. to Shattuck Ave. Go R 0.5 mi. to Channing Way, turn **L**. Drive 1 mi. to Channing's end at Prospect St and **L** on Prospect for one block.
Some 50 ft. south from the start of Panaramic Way you'll find Orchard Ln. consisting of several steep flights of stairs leading up to Mosswood Rd. A footpath also connects Mosswood to the stairway.

PARKING — Consider parking in the area of Channing and Prospect because continuing up Panaramic Way to Mosswood is difficult, norrow, and eventually dead-ended. In any case, it is necessary to walk the footpath for views of the house.

ACCESSIBILITY — This is a private residence.

PHOTOGRAPHY — The Mosswood side is heavily shaded, especially after the morning sun leaves. The views seen from the footpath have more light from midday on. Shots of the house are limited, but those from the footpath in the afternoon can be interesting.

Hilary and Joe Feldman House

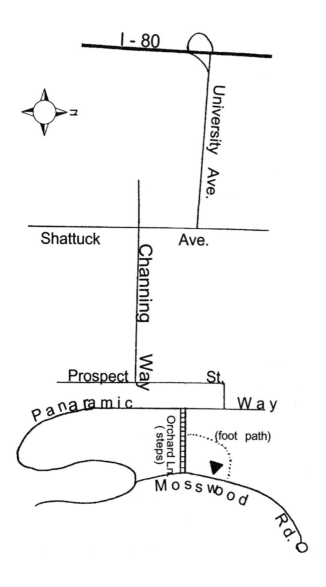

I - 80

University Ave.

Shattuck   Ave.

Channing Way

Prospect   St.

Panaramic   Way

Orchard Ln.
(steps)

(foot path)

M o s s w o o d

Rd.

Cameo 14

Wright worked in a manner unlike most architects, He did not take up his pencil to put plan on paper until he had virtually the entire concept and relationship of the spaces in his mind.

The story is told by his students and apprentices who witnessed how quickly he designed *Fallingwater*. It was several months after Edgar Kaufmann, Sr. had commissioned him to design a weekend retreat in a rustic mountain setting when the businessman phoned Wright at his *Taliesin* studio. He said he wanted to see what *the Master* had conjured up. He was in Milwaukee, not far away, and could be at *Taliesin* in about four hours. Wright told him to come right ahead and he would show him his plans.

Actually, nothing had yet been put on paper. Wright gathered his students around his drafting table. He began to produce plan, elevations, and sections and his apprentices finished renderings of the various views. In a mere two hours or so the fabulous structure took shape before their eyes.

"We've been waiting for you, Edgar," he tells Kaufmann on his arrival. The client saw quite clearly what *the Master* had conjured for his mountain haven and he was pleased by the stunning design.

Pilgrim Congregational Church

1958–63

□□□ The full design, one of Wright's last, was never realized. The completed structure is under a white metal roof lined with a natural wood ceiling. The exterior and interior walls are of rough stone. But its most distinctive feature is the angled and bent concrete stanchions supporting the roof which bring to mind the flying buttresses used on some centuries–old cathedrals. □□□

Pilgrim Congregational Church

2850 Foothill Blvd. — Redding

LOCATION — Redding is on I-5 some 170 mi. north of Sacramento.

DIRECTIONS — From I-5 – At the juncture of SR 299 and SR 44 turn west on SR 299 toward central Redding. Here it feeds into westbound Shasta St. West on Shasta 1.1 mi. to Almond Ave. Turn **R**, go 2 blocks to Foothill Blvd. then **L** to the address.

PARKING — The church lot can be used.

ACCESSIBILITY — If the church building is locked, the office is usually staffed during business hours. Someone there will be glad to show you around or allow you to visit the interior where you can see Wright's drawings.

PHOTOGRAPHY — No restrictions.

Pilgrim Congregational Church

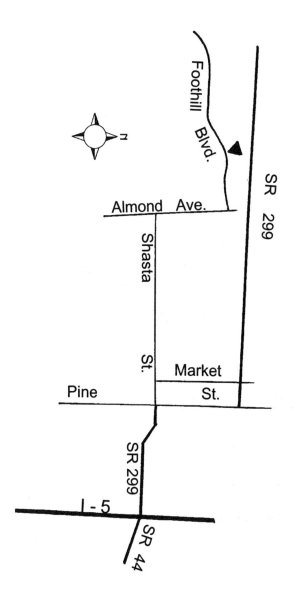

Foothill Blvd.

N

SR 299

Almond Ave.

Shasta St.

Market St.

Pine

SR 299

I - 5

SR 44

Cameo 15

At the turn of the century most Americans who traveled abroad went to Europe. On his first trip out of the country Wright went to Japan. He was enchanted by Japanese and other Asian art. He became an avid collector and was considered an expert. He even functioned as a dealer, selling to private collectors and museums.

It was this expertise that helped him get the commission for the Imperial Hotel in Tokyo. The Japanese government wanted a hotel built to Western standards to accommodate the growing numbers of businessmen starting to come from Western nations.

For more than five years most of Wright's time was spent in Japan supervising construction and designing details and furnishings. With the hotel virtually completed in 1922, he returned home. Just before the hotel's official opening, the Great Kanto Earthquake, Japan's biggest of the century, struck Tokyo. Thousands lost their lives. Radio and wire communications failed.

At his Wisconsin home Wright first heard reports that the hotel was destroyed. A few days later those reports proved to be false. Along with other substantially built buildings that had survived, the hotel still stood with minimal damage It was demolished in 1968. A reconstruction of its lobby entrance exists near Nagoya.

Ancillary Buildings

Some sites described in this book contain secondary structures that are either directly or indirectly related to Frank Lloyd Wright or to the principal building of the site. Five buildings located on four such sites are shown on this and the two following pages.

BARNSDALL SITE, p. 15 - "Residence A" guest house, 1921. Wright's design, with some modifications by R. M. Schindler. Now the Barnsdall Art Center.

Ancillary Buildings

MILLARD SITE, p. 11 - Studio-library addition by Lloyd Wright completed in 1926.

OBOLER SITE, p. 39 - The gatehouse, 1941.

Ancillary Buildings

MARIN COUNTY CIVIC CENTER, p. 63 - Veterans' Memorial Auditorium, completed 1972.

MARIN COUNTY CIVIC CENTER, p. 63 - U. S. Post Office, San Rafael California, Civic Center Branch.

Cameo 16

Frim the mid-1920s and through most of the Great Depression, Wright's output slowed. The architectural community assumed his career was ending. He was going into his sixties with over two hundred designs executed; a grand accomplishment for, essentially, a one-man shop.

But he reappeared on the horizon of American architecture with completion of *Fallingwater*, the residence which gained world renown. Then came the S. C. Johnson Wax Building, now one of he most visited commercial buildings. The name Frank Lloyd Wright was back in the limelight of world architecture. Now approaching his seventies, he would launch two more decades of phenomenal work.

Nearly another two hundred Wright designs took form, including the Guggenheim Museum in New York. Several of the designs he was working on at the end of his life were completed by Taliesin Architects, Ltd., a group associated with The Frank Lloyd Wright Foundation.

Wright was still working at the time of his death which came after a brief illness, in April 1959, two months short of his 92nd birthday. Originally interred near the small family chapel in Wisconsin he helped build as a youngster, he was later cremated and his ashes returned to Arizona at Mrs. Wright's request shortly before her death.

Table Of Contents

Wright In Arizona

Frank Lloyd Wright's first work in Arizona came about in the late 1920s, a few years after completing his work in Japan. He had tried unsuccessfully to establish himself in Los Angeles; then returned to his Wisconsin studio at a time when both his professional life and personal life were quite bleak.

But in 1929 two projects brought Wright back to the Southwest. One was the Arizona Biltmore Hotel in Phoenix on which he worked under contract to a former student of his. The second project was to be *San Marcos in the Desert,* a large resort complex at nearby Chandler. Wright moved a small group of assistants out from his Midwest headquarters to the project's property in the barren, open desert south of Phoenix and built a rustic and rudimentary camp he named Ocotillo. The timing was most unfortunate, because the financial crash of October 1929 that started the Great Depression doomed the project.

That rather brief stay in the desert camp must have agreed with Wright in many ways because a few years later he started building a second home and studio near Scottsdale. Like his earlier homes, the complex was continually being enlarged and modified. Taliesin West was a counterpart to his original Taliesin in Wisconsin. For the rest of his life the two served alternately as his winter and summer quarters. Today they continue to house the Frank Lloyd Wright Foundation.

Wright continued to design and build in many places throughout the country, but his new Arizona location no doubt played a part in his getting commissions for additional work in California as well as in the local area where, besides his studio-home, other works can be seen in Phoenix, Tempe and Scottsdale.

81

Visiting the Arizona Sites

Visiting Frank Lloyd Wright's work in Arizona can be done in one day or, a bit more leisurely, in a day and a half. This guide presents several options for the visitor.

Unlike the sites in California which are spread across the state, the Arizona locations are clustered in the Phoenix area, and so the presentation in this section is arranged differently. While the guide can be used to locate any of the sites individually, it also presents the entire group as a complete tour.

Six Wright-designed buildings are in the suggested tour that includes exterior viewing of two interesting residences and four sites open to visitors. While all the sites open to the public do offer guided tours, some require advance appointment. Times and conditions are stated in following pages.

DIRECTIONAL MAPS

Maps on next three pages show the general directional relationship of the six sites on a west- east axis. Distances and north-south relation- ships are distorted and not to scale.

Visiting the Arizona Sites

A good street map of the Phoenix area is helpful in finding your way to the starting points of the suggested routes or to the area of a specific site. It can also be helpful if you inadvertently stray from the route or encounter any detours. **Be aware that the circled "magnified view" maps show only streets useful in following the route and locating the site.**

The map at the bottom of these two pages is intended to show direction only. It does not depict distances accurately. Mileage between key points is stated in the detailed routing instructions.

The West-to-East Routing starts at Site #1 and ends at Site #6; the East-to-West Routing is the reverse. Which should you take?

It may depend on these factors:
□□ If you are scheduled for a morning tour at Taliesin West, you should tour East-to-West if you plan to see all sites in one day. Morning Taliesin tours, whether the standard one hour or one of the longer tours fit well with Gammage Auditorium tours that start at 1:00 p.m.

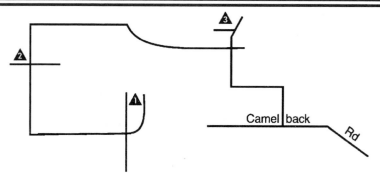

Visiting the Arizona Sites

⬜⬜ If you plan to do the Taliesin tour on a day by itself, it is best to start your tour of the other buildings at site No. 1

⬜⬜ If you are a total novice or only slightly conversant with Wright's work, it may be best to see Taliesin West first. in the morning, thus arriving at the Gammage close to its starting tour time.

⬜⬜ Remember that it is extremely hot in Phoenix in summertime. Taliesin discontinues afternoon tours in summer. Phone to verify tour hours.

You can, of course, visit any of these sites at your leisure during a longer stay in the area. But what if you are one of those "super-busy" folks? You may want to try what we call the "Fly in-Fly out Thing."

You fly in; do the tour; catch an evening plane back home or to your next destination. It depends on your available air schedules. You can do it from many major western cities and even places farther east which have a two or three hour jump on Phoenix time. You should arrive by at least 9 a.m. and pick up your reserved rental car.

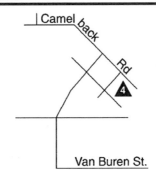

Visiting the Arizona Sites

From the airport go north a mile or so on Interstate10 to the interchange; then continue north on Route 51 about seven miles. (It's called Northwest Ave. through Phoenix Mountain Preserve.) Proceed another mile and a half to Shea Blvd. and turn **right**. Drive east 10 miles to 114th St., turning **left** there onto Frank Lloyd Wright Blvd, as shown on the Site # 6 Map. After your tour of Taliesin West you can follow the East to West Routing as shown in the guide.

To return to the airport from the last site, the Arizona Biltmore Hotel, 24th St. south runs right to it, as do Routes 51 and I-10, the ones you started out on. Route 51 is a half mile west of 24th St.

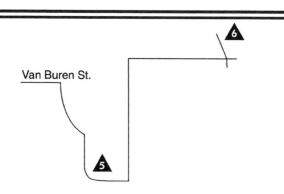

Van Buren St.

West to East Tour Route

THIS ROUTE BEGINS at the Arizona Biltmore Hotel located on 24th St. at Missouri Ave. in Phoenix. 24th St. is 5 mi. east of Route 17 (Black Canyon Highway). Missouri Ave. is about 4 mi. north of Interstate 10.

To Site #1 - ARIZONA BILTMORE HOTEL - The entrance to Arizona Biltmore Hotel and Country Club is on the east side of 24th St., where Missouri Ave. ends. Enter and follow the drive about half a mile. There are signs leading to the hotel, which will be to your left. You can self-park beyond the entrance areas.

To Site #2 - FIRST CHRISTIAN CHURCH - From the hotel entrance on 24th St., drive directly west on Missouri Ave. Continue past 7th St.. and beyond Central Ave. to SEVENTH AVENUE and turn **R**. Drive north on Seventh to Ocotillo Rd. (6700).

To Site #3 - NORMAN LYKES HOUSE - From the church go north two blocks and turn **R** onto Glendale Ave. which becomes Lincoln Dr. Continue on Lincoln to 36th St. (also signed as Palo Christi). Turn **L** on 36th, go about half a mile to where the house is in view at Nepthane Dr.

To Site #4 - DAVID WRIGHT HOUSE - From the Lykes house return to Lincoln and continue south on 36th to Stanford Dr.; turn **L** to 44th St. and turn **R**. Go south on 44th to Camelback Rd. and turn **L**. Proceed to Rubicon Ave. (one block past traffic light at Arcadia Dr.). The house is viewed from Rubicon just north Exitor Ave.

To Site #5 - GRADY GAMMAGE MEMORIAL AUDITORIUM - From Rubicon and Exitor turn back (west) one block on Exiter to Arcadia and turn **L**, cross the water channel and continue to Indian School Rd. (The shortest way from here to the Gammage is as follows, but see alternative routes on the next page): A short jog **L** lets you turn onto and run south on 48th St. (If necessitated by detours, use 44th St., not secondary streets to the east.) Turn **L** on Van Buren St. which becomes Mill Rd. in Papago Park and runs through the business

West to East Tour Route

district near the university. If you wish lunch now, there are restaurants in this area. The Gammage is visible where Mill Rd. turns left into Apache Rd. Take any of the access drives leading to the parking areas of the Auditorium. Parking is free.

To Site #6 - TALIESIN WEST - From the auditorium exit the parking area onto Mill Rd. and/or Apache Rd. and proceed east about a mile to Rural Rd. and turn **L**. Drive 11.5 mi. north on Rural and Scottsdale Roads to Shea Blvd. Turn **R** and continue about 5.5 mi. east to 114th St. where a **L** turn puts you on Frank Lloyd Wright Blvd. Drive 1.2 mi. to the entrance of the Taliesin West gate. Enter the private road and proceed to the parking areas.

Alternative Routes

After viewing the David Wright House, if you wish to go directly to Taliesin West. (since afternoon tours are curtailed in summer) proceed as stated in Alt.Route (a), below.
To go directly to the Gammage is given in Alt.Route (b).

ALT. ROUTE (a) - To TALIESIN - Return to Camelback Rd. and go east to Scottsdale Rd. Turn **L** and drive north to Shea Blvd. Continue as stated above for reaching Site #6.

To visit the Gammage after Taliesin, retrace your route on Shea Blvd and Scottsdale Rd, continuing straight down to Apache Rd. and turn **R**. Go aout a mile to where Apache turns north into Mill Rd. and exit onto any of the access drives leading to the Auditorium and parking areas.

ALT. ROUTE (b) - To GAMMAGE AUDITORIUM from the David Wright house. Return to Camelback Rd.and continue east to Scottsdale Rd. Turn **R** and go south to Apache Rd and turn **R**. Go about a mile to where Apache turns north into Mill Rd. and exit onto any of the access drives leading to the Auditorium and parking area.

Site Location Maps

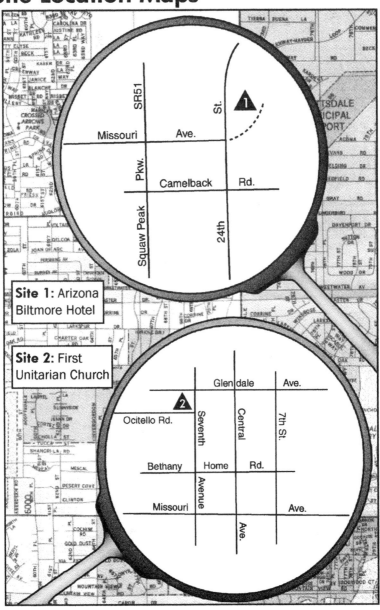

Site 1: Arizona Biltmore Hotel

Site 2: First Unitarian Church

Site Location Maps

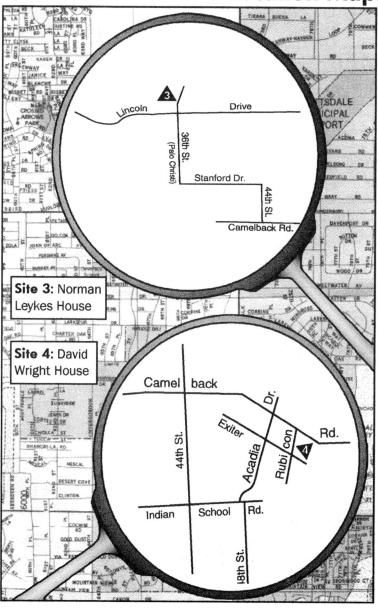

Site 3: Norman Leykes House

Site 4: David Wright House

Site Location Maps

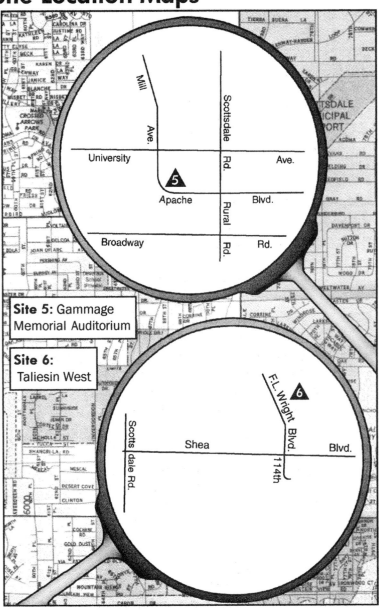

Site 5: Gammage Memorial Auditorium

Site 6: Taliesin West

East to West Tour Route

THIS ROUTE BEGINS at Wright's Arizona home and studio, located on the northeast fringe of the Phoenix metropolitan area in Scottsdale. It is approached via Shea Blvd., an east-west main thoroughfare about ten miles to the north of the I -10 in the downtown Phoenix area. For visitors unfamiliar with the area, Shea Blvd. is most easily reached using either Rt. 51 (Squaw Park Parkway) or Scottsdale Rd., a few miles east.

To Site #6 - TALIESIN WEST - Once on Shea Blvd., drive east to 114th St. Turn **L** here onto Frank Lloyd Wright Blvd. Proceed 1.2 mi. to the gate of Taliesin West. Turn **R** and continue on the private road to the parking area. [If you are doing the "Fly in - Fly out Thing" see page 86 for directions from the airport to Site #6 .]

To Site #5 - GAMMAGE MEMORIAL AUDITORIUM - From Taliesin, return west on Shea Blvd. 5.5 mi. to Scottsdale Rd., turn **L** and drive south (becomes Rural Rd in Tempe). At Apache Rd, turn **R**, proceed one mile to where it swings north into Mill Rd. Use any of the access drives leading to auditorium parking areas at your right.

To Site #4 - DAVID WRIGHT HOUSE - From the Gammage, drive north on Mill Rd. which turns west through Papago Park and becomes Van Buren St. Drive to 48th St. (alternatively, 44th St.), turn R and run north to Indian School Rd. Just a jog west of the Indian School and 48th juncture, (or about two blocks east of 44th), pick up Arcadia Dr. Go north about one mile to Exitor Ave; turn **R**. One block east is Rubicon Ave.; turn **L**. The house is seen from the driveway a short way up Rubicon.

91

East to West Tour Route

To Site #3 - NORMAN LYKES HOUSE - From the Wright house, continue up Rubicon turning **L** onto Camelback Rd. Drive to 44th St., turn **R**. then turn **L** on Stanford and **R** onto Palo Christi (36th St.). Drive north on 36th St., crossing Lincoln Dr. and continuing 1.2 mi. to Nepthane Dr. where the house can be seen.

To Site #2 - FIRST CHRISTIAN CHURCH - From the Lykes house return to Lincoln Dr. and turn **R**. (Lincoln becomes Glendale Ave.) Continue to Seventh Avenue (not 7th St.). Turn **L** to the church at Ocotillo Rd - two blocks.

To Site #1 - ARIZONA BILTMORE HOTEL - From the church drive south on Seventh Avenue to Missouri Ave., turn **L** and continue to its end at 24th St. Entrance to the Arizona Biltmore Hotel and Country Club is directly ahead. Follow the private drive about half a mile. There are signs directing to the hotel which will be at your left. You can self-park beyond the entrance area.

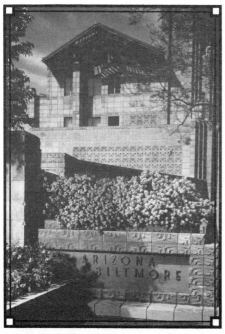

Arizona Biltmore Hotel
1927

24th St. and Missouri Ave, Phoenix

□□□ We include in the Arizona works of Frank Lloyd Wright the Arizona Biltmore Hotel despite the fact that he did not claim authorship of the work.The architect of record is Albert McArthur, formerly a Wright apprentice in Oak Park, whose brothers financed the project.

According to one senario, Wright was hired as consultant on the use of his "textile concrete block" system. It is difficult to envision him in so passive a roll on any project. Some writers and historians feel that Wright was much more actively involved, though contractually bound to deny it.

In his comprehensive Wright catalog, William A. Storrer flatly states: "Both the hotel and cottages are Wright's work." Donald Hoppen, a former Wright student and a professor of architecture, writes: "Wright's signature is everywhere apparent." In Meryle Secrest's biography of Wright she lists many features that "bear the stamp of Wright's personality" and quotes from his letter to McArthur's widow where he wrote: "The whole office knew how the building came to be as it is...nevertheless I have always given Albert's name as architect...but I know better and so should you."

You can decide for yourself as to his involvement. But a visitor to Phoenix wishing to see Wright's works that are there to be seen must visit the Arizona Biltmore. We point out that it is a resort hotel with rates commensurate with that type of establishment. Information is available at (602) 954-7000. But you need not be a registered guest to wander through the grounds and public areas of the hotel. Photography is permitted. Private guided tours can be arranged.

Our suggested west-to-east tour route begins at the hotel. The east-to-west routing ends there. □□□

First Christian Church
1973

6570 N. Seventh Avenue, Phoenix

□□□ Designed by Wright in 1950, it was built after his death by the Taliesin Associated Architects group. A urethane roof instead of the intended copper covers a structure of rough desert stone. The stained glass window is by Taliesin artist John Amarantides.

Do not confuse Seventh Avenue, which is a mile west of Central Avenue, with 7th St., to the east. To visit the interior if it is not open for its many daily activities, ask at the church office if they will allow access. Guided tours (8:30 a.m. to 5 p.m.) are by appointment only. Call 602-246-9206. □□□

Norman Lykes House

1968

6836 North 36th St., Phoenix

□□□ Wright's last residential design (done in 1959) was
built of concrete block under supervision of a Taliesin
Fellow who added an upper-floor studio. So many circular lines are not often seen in a Wright residence. They
are quite a departure from the rectangularity of the *Prairie
House* style of his early career.

The broad-spanning house almost appears to have been
chiseled out of the rough-faced mountain it is set on.□□□

David Wright House

1950   ▲4

5212 East. Exiter Rd., Phoenix

□□□ This address does not appear on Exiter Rd. and the house cannot be seen from that street. You see it from the Rubicon Ave. side where a driveway enters the property and, oddly, the mailbox still bears the 5212 house number.

Wright designed this house for his son David. Here he employs not only his late-career affinity for circles but also a favorite device for joining different levels - the ramp.

The original plot was later subdivided and three houses were built on the Exiter frontage. The house directly to the south, which fronts on Exiter Rd., was built for Wright's grandson and was designed by his uncle Lloyd Wright. □□□

Grady Gammage
Memorial Auditorium
1964

Apache Blvd. and Mill Avenue, Tempe

□□□ Wright's last non-residential design is on the campus of Arizona State University. Seating 3000, it serves the school and the community as an auditorium, theater and concert hall. It also contains classrooms for the university's performing arts students. □□□

For better acoustics, the grand tier between orchestra and balcony stands free of the rear wall and is supported by a 145 foot girder, one of the longest such spans ever used in a structure. Fifty concrete pillars, 55 feet tall, support the roof.

Inquire at the box office about the free tours offered 1:00 p.m. to 3:30 p.m. except during performances or other scheduled events.

Taliesin West

1937-56

12621 Frank Lloyd Wright Blvd. Scottsdale

□□□ In 1937, after an earlier short stay in the desert east of Phoenix, Wright returned to establish a second home, a place where he could work and where his Taliesin Fellowship could function away from the rigorous Wisconsin winters.

Walls were made from colorful desert rock imbedded in concrete. Originally, redwood-framed stretched canvas also served as wall and ceiling panels. Today steel framing and fiberglass are in place.

Wright took his architectural theme from the saw-toothed silhouettes of the surrounding mountains. The buildings are low, slant-roofed, with tilted walls - an example of Wright's flair for fitting the structure to the site.

The Frank Lloyd Wright School of Architecture continues here in the tradition of the original Taliesin Fellowship. The Frank Lloyd Wright Foundation is also headquartered here.

The Bruce Brooks Pfeiffer residence which stands at the edge of Taliesin was completed in 1974. It is sometimes made available to visitors on the more extensive tours. ▫▫▫

Cameo 17

Frank Lloyd Wright designed over a thousand structures. While most were commissioned by clients, Wright also designed a number of speculative projects. Often they were to present a principle or theory of his. And there were some spectacular commissioned projects where the clients failed to follow through.

His famous *Broadacre City* was an exercise in urban planning based on the concept that future cities should be spread horizontally rather than in congested vertical growth. His model was exhibited around the country.

An unusual project was the Gordon Strong Automobile Objective, a structure forming a circular drive atop the crest of Sugarloaf Mountain in Maryland, intended simply as a vista point with a planetarium at the top.

Pittsburgh Point was intended as the civic center for Pittsburgh at the juncture where two rivers form the Ohio. He designed two massive spans to join the adjacent shores to where the center would be situated at the point where the rivers merge..

These and others show the broad range in which Wright could work, but none would be more in the realm of fantasy than *The Illinois*, proposed as the State's government center. It would be a building of 528 stories: yes, 5280 feet, or one mile high!

Notes

Site List

The Wright Places in California

PASADENA	ALICE MILLARD HOUSE
LOS ANGELES	ALINE BARNSDALL HOUSE *
LOS ANGELES	CHARLES ENNIS HOUSE *
HOLLYWOOD	SAMUEL FREEMAN HOUSE
HOLLYWOOD	JOHN STORER HOUSE
BEVERLY HILLS	ANDERTON COURT SHOPS +
BRENTWOOD	GEORGE D. STURGES HOUSE
MALIBU	ARCH OBOLER STUDIO & GATEHOUSE
MONTECITO	GEORGE C. STEWART HOUSE
SAN LUIS OBISPO	KENDERT MEDICAL CLINIC +
CARMEL	CLINTON WALKER HOUSE
PALO ALTO	PAUL and JEAN HANNA HOUSE *
SAN FRANCISCO	V. C. MORRIS GIFT SHOP +
SAN RAFAEL	MARIN COUNTY CIVIC CENTER * +
BERKELEY	HILARY and JOE FELDMAN HOUSE
REDDING	PILGRIM CONGREGATIONAL CHURCH +

The Wright Places in Arizona

PHOENIX	ARIZONA BILTMORE HOTEL *+
	FIRST CHRISTIAN CHURCH *
	NORMAN LYKES HOUSE
	DAVID WRIGHT HOUSE
TEMPE	GRADY GAMMAGE MEMORIAL AUDITORIUM *
SCOTTSDALE	TALIESIN WEST *

* Sites where scheduled or special tours are offered.
+ Buildings generally open to the public .

104